HAIKU
PEOPLE

HAIKU
PEOPLE

BIG AND SMALL
IN POEMS AND PRINTS

By Stephen Addiss

with Fumiko
and Akira Yamamoto

NEW YORK WEATHERHILL TOKYO

First edition, 1998

Published by Weatherhill, Inc.
568 Broadway, Suite 705
New York, New York 10012

© 1998 by Stephen Addiss

Library of Congress Cataloging-in-Publication Data

Addiss, Stephen, 1935–
    Haiku people, big and small : in poems and prints /
    by Stephen Addiss with Fumiko and Akira
    Yamamoto. — 1st ed.
            p.   cm
        ISBN 0–8348–0417–4
            1. Haiku — Translations into English.
    I. Yamamoto, Fumiko Y.   II. Yamamoto, Akira Y.
    III. Title.
    PL782.E3 A23   1998
    895.6' 104108—dc21   97–51890
                                                        CIP

Printed in Hong Kong

CONTENTS

Dedicated to
Fukushima Keidô Rôshi

Multiple Interpretations

> New Year's day—
> no good, no bad
> just people
>   *Shiki*

Welcome to *Haiku People*. This volume was conceived because our two previous books, *A Haiku Menagerie* and *A Haiku Garden,* suggested a third, dealing with the most important theme not yet covered: human beings. People appear everywhere in haiku and Japanese woodblock book illustrations, big and small, serious and funny, handsome and ugly, rich and poor, working and playing, and above all marvelously full of life.

Our initial question in preparing this volume was how to organize haiku poems and woodblock prints that deal with people—the young, the old, and everyone in between. It would have been easy to use the four seasons as in *A Haiku Garden,* since Japanese haiku contain seasonal reference words called *kigo,* but instead we decided to follow the natural cycle of human life from childhood through maturity to old age. In this way we could chart a lifespan, with the different interests, joys, and sorrows that occur from birth to death. The ability of fine poets and artists to see the world through the eyes of the child, the mature, and the old is remarkable. At the same time, they demonstrate a unique gift for experiencing the wondrous in the everyday world and expressing it with sensitivity and imagination.

The sense of discovery we find in haiku can come through the poet's own experience, or it can be the result of empathy, as in a modern haiku by Chiba Hiroshi:

> The naked child
> delighted by my
> nakedness

Brief as it is, the haiku is not limited to single emotions. The greatest poet of children and other small creatures was Kobayashi Issa. Remembering his own beloved child who had died tragically young, Issa combines the pang of memory, the passage of time, his child's delight in flowers, and the poet's own mirroring of this delight, all within three short lines:

> Autumn wind
> my child wanted to pick
> these red flowers

Haiku can also come directly from a child's discovery of the world. The writer Atoda Ko wrote in the *Asahi* newspaper on January 21, 1996 that his child noticed how the cherry trees seem to bloom fully in a single night, saying, "Last night, blossoms climbed to the top of the trees!" This act of perception entranced the child, but we adults can also be moved by a sense of empathy, as we are when we read this poem by third grader Haneda Koji:

> Scolding father,
> me being scolded
> both sweating

Children also seem to have a fresh eye for everyday experience. First grader Atarashi Miyuki wrote, after a visit to the hospital:

> My grandpa
> attached to an I.V.
> I wipe off his sweat

In contrast to childhood, maturity brings poems of romance, of pursuing one's goals in the world, and of raising a family. The delicate hue of young love is captured by a poet of three hundred yeas ago:

> First love
> close to a lantern
> face to face
> *Tan Taigi*

The sorrows of failed romance are equally represented in haiku, here by the modern poet Fujita Shoshi:

> Not being loved
> I swim
> far into the sea

Less dramatic, but no less perceptive, is a haiku by the master Yosa Buson:

> I prepared sushi
> having no one special
> to wait for

The poet Oikawa Sada expresses a sadness unique to a parent, the loss of a child before he could savor the full scope of life:

> Deep into the rainy season—
> a child lost in the war
> without knowing love

Old age, with its contentment and quietude, the bittersweet pleasures of solitude, and finally the confrontation with death, has a special place in haiku. Naka Kansuke delicately suggests these feelings in his poem:

> A solitary game of *go*
> on a day when powdery snow
> piles on the bamboo

Perhaps the most distinctive quality acquired by many people in their final years is an ability to look upon the world of life and death with a refreshing honesty:

> This body, to be given
> for medical research
> is flower viewing
> *Kubota Asako*

We can enjoy each precious moment right here, right now, says this haiku, no matter what awaits us after death.

While the woodblock prints we have included clearly depict people in different stages of life, haiku are subject to multiple interpretations, and the age of the human subject in a poem is not always clear. In assigning certain poems to a section, we have risked the danger of attaching to it one particular interpretation among many, and in a way limiting or diminishing its full range of possible meanings. For example, this verse by Shōhaku definitely suggests the season of summer when the cuckoo is first heard:

> Cuckoo
> but just for today
> no one is here

But several interpretations are possible. Is this cuckoo a messenger of love, as was typical in early Japanese court poetry? If so, this is the verse of a young adult, longing for the beloved. But the poem might also suggest that as the years go by, one loses one's companions, making it a poem of old age. One of the joys of haiku, in fact, is the multiple interpretations that each poem suggests. When you encounter a poem that is especially resonant, you should try to imagine several meanings for it. This is what makes reading haiku such a rich and participative experience.

It might seem at first that we humans, with our broad range of backgrounds, professions, ages, emotions, personalities, and peculiarities, would offer the richest source of haiku subjects, but since Japanese haiku usually have a natural theme, humans often enter the poems only as secondary figures. Yet here, too, haiku leave much room for interpretation. One question we faced when selecting haiku was whether a poem was an observation of nature or an evocation of humanity. Those living near the sea in cold climates can easily share the haiku experience of the novelist Natsume Sōseki:

Tree-withering wind
shakes the setting sun
into the ocean

Is this a poem entirely about nature, or is there a human aspect implied with-
in it? The elements are natural, but the perception of the wind shaking the sun
is certainly personal. Another example of this ambiguity can be found in a
poem by the early master Shintoku:

Wild geese
falling right down my neck
frosty night

Shintoku observes the geese, but it is the perception that they seem to head-
ing directly towards him as they descend from the sky that gives the haiku its
resonance. A poem by Issa presents a more subtle question about its subject:

Clear morning
the charcoal crackles
cheerfully

On the surface, this haiku seems to merely observe the charcoal, but the last line
suggests a human emotion, leading us to inquire whether the poem is really about
the charcoal at all, or rather about the mood of the poet in the brisk morning weather.
Perhaps we should not argue this point; the haiku moment may arrive most fully
when such concerns fade away. The poet is the charcoal, and the charcoal is the poet.

A final example, from one of the modern masters of haiku, is even more
suggestive and terse, consisting of only three words in both the original
Japanese and our English translation:

Cold
clouds
hurrying
Santōka

Are the clouds hurrying? Or is hurrying strictly a human perception? Or might the clouds be the observers, watching the poet, a begging monk, hurrying on his way?

These questions of interpretation are one of the reasons why it is so fascinating to read and translate Japanese haiku. They seem to convey a multitude of meanings not despite but rather because of their brevity. It is not just brevity, however, that allows this form to speak so richly. The haiku technique of projecting emotion through natural imagery instead of stating it directly contributes enormously to the expressive power of the poems. It may be our own cheerfulness, our hurriedness, that the last two poems express, but somehow these feelings become both more personal and more universal when transposed to our perceptions of a charcoal fire or clouds.

It is this unique sense of perception that is central to the haiku aesthetic. When we are merely feeling, our emotions are limited to ourselves. When they are allied with perception, however, they can become shared, and this is the joy of a fine haiku. Bashō did not merely observe a frog jumping into an old pond. He focused his attention upon the event so strongly that everyone reading his poem is right there with him, listening to the sound of water as though for the first time.

This balance between the natural world and human nature is precisely what can make haiku about people so charming and insightful. If the poems were too human they could become egoistic. One of the secrets of fine haiku is that the poet does not give primacy to a direct expression of his or her emotion. We have to intuit what Bashō or Shintoku is feeling. The clues are contained within the haiku, but the final interpretation is up to each one of us, limited only by our own ability to empathize.

Is it strange that these little poems demand so much of us? Great narrative epics from other cultures ask for our sustained attention, and perhaps even our sympathy, but it is the tiny haiku that requires our fullest participation. The significance of a haiku comes not just from the poet, but from our own experience, our understanding, and our acceptance of the entire world around us.

In addition to the interpretive challenge inherent to haiku, we English readers face an additional hurdle: we must read the poems in translation. There have been a number of different approaches to rendering haiku into English, each with its own values. One method has been to use rhyme at the end of the first and third lines. This adds a sense of structure, but it can seem forced unless it is done with consummate skill, and it may foster a serious misunderstanding of haiku, since there is no rhyme in the original Japanese poems.

A second approach has been to maintain the 5–7–5 syllable count that appears in the originals. This has many advantages, but the one major problem is that it often requires extra syllables in English to make up for longer words in Japanese. Here, for example, is a word-for-word rendering of Bashō's most famous haiku, indicating that the original does not distinguish singular or plural cases:

Furu ike ya	Old pond(s) (pause)
kawazu tobikomu	frog(s) jump(s)/dive(s) in
mizu no oto	water('s) sound

In this case maintaining a 5–7–5 syllable count necessitates adding words to the Japanese. Possibilities for a five-syllable first line might be: "There is an old pond" or "At an ancient pond," while a seven-syllable second line could be: "from the banks a frog jumps in" or "suddenly a frog jumps in." The problem is that these extra words add elements not explicitly stated by Bashō, diluting the power of the poem's expression. Our approach, therefore, has generally been too avoid using more syllables than the 5–7–5 form, but not to be afraid of shortening the syllable count if doing so eliminates padding.

A third approach is to try to improve the original poems when rendering them into English. For example, in the final line of the Bashō poem, some translators have decided that the single syllable "splash" or "plop" enhances the effect. Perhaps so, but Japanese has many more onomatopoetic words than English, and Bashō did not choose to use one. Doing so in English changes the poem, even if the translator thinks that's what Bashō meant.

A fourth approach, more appealing but ultimately pernicious, has been to translate the putative *meaning* of the poem, rather than what the poem says. Due to the nature of the two languages, sometimes this cannot be avoided, but it leads to interpretive problems for the translator. For example, there is no way to be certain from the original text whether Bashō intended either a single pond or a single frog. In this case, we seem to have general agreement that one pond and one frog make for the strongest image, but in other cases there are various opinions about singular and plural, including that both possibilities should coexist. Translators into English don't have both options. We must choose singular or plural, adding an element of interpretation and cutting off some possible meanings.

For Japan's most famous poem, we can easily preserve the five syllables of Bashō's final line, since that is natural to the text, but the English version given here shortens the first two lines to focus upon the words that Bashō used.

Furu ike ya	Old pond
kawazu tobikomu	a frog jumps in
mizu no oto	the sound of water

There are different interpretive possibilities even for such a celebrated (and seemingly simple) poem. For example, does the haiku suggest a sequence of events or perceptions in which there is first a pond, then a diving frog, and then the sound of water? Or does the poem express a single moment in which the pond, frog, and sound are simultaneous? The poet Sam Hamill has taken this approach, translating the final two lines as "a frog plunges into / the sound of water." Changing these few words transforms the haiku, and this is the joy, and sometimes the despair, of the translator.

To make matters more difficult, there are many cases when Japanese readers would clearly understand a meaning not directly stated in the text, for example, a reference to a certain festival, or to the seasons. In these cases translators may feel obligated to add something not directly stated, because the alternative is to explain the poem after the translation is completed, not a happy task. However, there are many other cases when it is not necessary to interpret in the translation, even when the translator believes that the poem suggests a meaning that it does not directly state. The difficult but fascinating challenge is to stick closely to the text and still convey as many of the subtleties of the original as possible.

Adhering to the text is not always easy, and there are even disputes about the proper format for haiku in translation. One authority has suggested that haiku should be translated in one continuous line, arguing that the original Japanese is a single unit without line breaks. Most translators, however, prefer the three-line format, which often helps suggest multiple interpretations through the spatial rhythm of the poem's visual presentation. A well-known poem by Buson offers a chance to compare continuity to multiplicity. Here is a word-for-word translation:

Yanagi chiri	Willow(s) bare
shimizu kare	clear stream(s) dried up
ishi tokoro dokoro	rock(s) here and there

There is a tendency when translating this kind of a poem, in which each line stands alone, to tie them together with verbs or prepositions:

> Bare willows stand
> where the dried up clear stream
> shows scattered rocks

Buson, however, deliberately avoided connecting words and altered the usual 5–7–5 syllable pattern to 5–5–8, giving extra emphasis to the final line.

Since the images in his poem emerge like separate, irregularly shaped rocks in the bed of a stream, isn't a direct translation ultimately more flavorful? Even here, however, the translator has choices in word order and line length:

Willows bare	Bare willows
clear stream dried up	dried up stream
rocks scattered here and there	scattered rocks

Which do you prefer?

The two versions have different impacts. The second is much terser. Yet they are alike in presenting the three images without interpretation.

In the world of haiku, it is often up to the reader to make the connection between lines, and ultimately this strengthens the poem, even if at first it does not read as smoothly or quickly. A haiku may be a sentence, part of a sentence, sections of several sentences, or merely images floating in the air. It is up to the translator to follow the text when the original haiku avoids specifics of grammar that would fix a single meaning to the poem. It seems to be a Western characteristic to try to get at *the* meaning, as though any fine work of art has a single specific meaning that we can find and define. Here is our chance, through haiku, to open our perceptions and enrich our tolerance for multiplicity.

Ultimately, every translation is partial and temporary, because none can suggest all the meanings implicit in the original Japanese poems, much less equal their verbal music. We have attempted to avoid changing, supplementing, or over-interpreting the poems we have included here. Even so, some of the music of the original is unavoidably lost, and those who read Japanese are invited to read the haiku in the original, to listen to the original sounds of the syllables, and to feel their rhythms. Then, if you wish, make your own translation. This is what we all do internally every time we read a poem or view a work of art, since ultimately the most important translation is from words and images to human experience. And despite the increased reliance upon technology in both Japan and the West as the century reaches its end, human experience also continues to give birth to haiku:

> Old pond paved over
> into a parking lot
> one frog still singing
> *Stephen Addiss*

The Woodblock Prints

Japanese prints are perhaps the most popular form of East Asian art in the world, but it is only the single-sheet prints of such masters as Harunobu, Hokusai, and Hiroshige that are famous. Artists not only of the *ukiyo-e* tradition, but of many different styles and schools, provided paintings and sketches for woodblock reproduction, and we have chosen masters whose work seems to express the same spirit as the haiku. These works by artists of the seventeenth to early twentieth centuries suggest more than they define, and they offer the viewer the opportunity to explore both the outer world of Japanese society and the inner world of feelings and emotions that cross geographical barriers to present themselves today as fresh evocations of human experience.

The prints in this volume are not *haiga,* the combination of poem and painting into a single work of art. Instead, we have presented prints and poems that express views of the progression from youth to old age, in the hope that the visual and verbal images may resonate together. We have included a great variety of artists and artistic styles. For example, there are several works by Hanabusa Itchō, who trained in the official Kanō School, the painting academy that dominated official commissions from the government from 1615 to 1868. The woodblock designs by Itchō show his mastery of the Chinese-derived ink-painting style, but also display his personal wit and humor. In contrast, the figures by Yamaguchi Soken were drawn a century later in a more relaxed brushwork typical of the naturalistic Maruyama-Shijō School, and yet they have an equal touch of gentle humor.

Kamisaka Sekka lived into the modern era of Japan, but followed the traditional Rimpa (decorative) School in art. He was a master of many media, creating not only paintings and prints but also designs for lacquer, furniture, ceramics, and textiles. His greatest achievement may have come, however, in his woodblock books, which are truly splendid in both design and production. Underneath the sumptuous presentation, however, we can still sense an approach to the figure similar to that seen in the works of Itchō and Soken, combining artistic skill at capturing a variety of ages, professions, activities, and personalities with an inner smile at human foibles.

Like haiku poets, Japanese artists have been able to offer their perceptions with a sharp eye while viewing humanity with interest, empathy, and amused tolerance. Perhaps they are suggesting that we focus our attention better when we do not take ourselves too seriously, and that we can see both others and ourselves more clearly when we experience the moments of everyday life with fresh vision:

A long day
he left after passing on
his yawns to me

CHILDHOOD

Traces of school ink
on his lips, a child enjoys
the evening cool
Senna

唇に
墨つく児の
すずみかな
千那

Testing
by stepping out—
the ice is thin
Haritsu

試みに
踏めば氷の
薄きかな
杷栗

Searching for
the lost child
with his own drum
Anonymous

迷い子の
おのが太鼓で
たずねられ

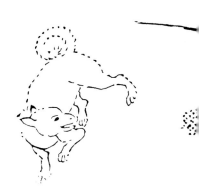

Counting flea bites
while she nurses
her baby
Issa

蚤のあと
かぞえながらに
添乳かな
一茶

The child lulled to sleep,
she washes its clothes—
summer moon
Issa

ねせつけし
子の洗たくや
夏の月
一茶

The mother eats
the bitter parts—
mountain persimmons
Issa

しぶいとこ
母がくいけり
山の柿
一茶

When the first
grandchild arrives, everything
becomes dangerous
Toshiko

初孫が

出来てあぶない

ことばかり

とし子

Garden butterfly—
as the baby crawls, it flies
crawls close, flies on
Issa

庭の蝶

子が這えば飛び

這えば飛び

一茶

Asked his age
he hold up one hand—
summer clothes

Issa

年とえば

片手だす子や

ころもがえ

一茶

A small child
eating all alone—
autumn dusk
Shōhaku

おさな子や

一人めし喰う

秋の暮れ

尚白

Furious rain—
even the crying child
is silenced
Anonymous

酷い降り

泣いていた子も

黙るなり

Today too!
today too! Kites
  caught by the nettle tree
                    Issa

今 日 も 今 日 も

凧 き っ か か る

榎 か な

        一 茶

Wives and children
eating in the temple—
early winter storm
Buson

妻も子も
寺でもの喰う
野わきかな
　　蕪村

The youngest child
visiting family graves
carries the broom
Buson

末の子や

お墓参りの

ほうきもち

蕪村

Spring river—
a tiny wooden clog
floats by
Haritsu

春の川

小さな下駄の

流れ行く

杷栗

The toddler—
as he laughs
autumn evening
Issa

おさなごや

笑うにつけて

秋の暮れ

一茶

Like the beauty of
boys soon to take the tonsure—
poppy flowers
Issa

僧になる

うつくしや

けしの花

一茶

Letting the child
on my back hold some bracken
I just picked

Gyōtai

負うた子に
蕨をとりて
もたせけり
　　暁台

"Give me
that harvest moon"
cries the child
Issa

名月を
とってくれろと
泣く子かな

一茶

Though she can watch
her child gathering seashells—
the mother worries

Anonymous

見通しに

いるのに汐干

母案じ

Given fireworks
he prays for the sun
to go down, go down
Anonymous

花火を
貰い日がくれろ
日がくれろ

The new father
sings the lullabye
out of tune
Anonymous

亭主のは
節のちがった
こもりうた

The tiny child
shown a flower
opens its mouth
Seifu-jo

おさなごや
花を見せても
くちをあく

星布女

Worse than tears—
the smile of the
abandoned child
Anonymous

泣くよりも
あわれ捨て子の
笑い顔

Stretching her arms
to form a peony—
"It's this big!"
Issa

これほどの
ぼたんと仕かた
する子かな
一茶

Despite the morning frost—
a child
selling flowers
Issa

朝霜や
しかも子どもの
お花売
一茶

Heaven knows,

earth knows, neighbors know—

parents don't know

Shishōshi

天知る

地知る近所知る

親知らず

而笑子

Melting snow
fills the village
with children
Issa

雪とけて
村いっぱいの
子供かな
一茶

Exhausted by
the crowd of children—
a sparrow
Issa

大ぜいの
子に疲れたる
雀かな
一茶

Shielding an infant
from the autumn wind—
a scarecrow

Issa

ち の み ご の
風 除 け に た つ
か か し か な
一 茶

Spring rain—
a child teaches its cat
to dance

Issa

春 雨 や
猫 に 踊 り を
教 え る 子
一 茶

Fleeing people,
getting used to people—
baby sparrows

Onitsura

人 に 逃 げ
人 に な る る や
雀 の 子
鬼 貫

The season's first melon
clutched in its arms—
the child sleeps
Issa

初瓜を
ひっとらまえて
寝た子かな
一茶

Blazing sun—
whose barefoot child
is running free?
Kōyō

炎天や
誰が子裸足の
放し飼い
紅葉

Morning glories—
on little feet
flea bites
Kitō

朝顔や
稚き足に
蚤のあと
几董

First kimono—
may you quickly grow to
a naughty age

Issa

初袷
にくまれ盛りに
はやくなれ

一茶

Heat shimmers—
clinging to my eyes
is that smiling face
Issa

陽炎や
目につきまとう
わらい顔
　　一茶

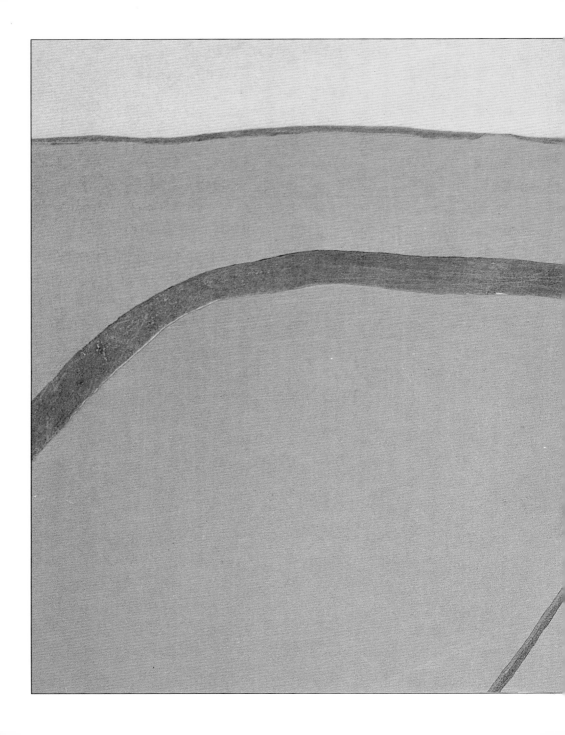

MATURITY

Harvesting radishes,
he points the way
with a radish
Issa

大根引
大根で道を
教えけり
一茶

For me leaving
for you staying
two autumns
Buson

行くに我に
とどまるなれに
秋二つ
蕪村

Polishing mirrors
he bends over
his own face
Anonymous

かがみとぎ
おのれが顔へ
のしかかり

Spring breeze
a pipe in his mouth—
the boatman
Bashō

春風や
煙管くはえて
船どどの
芭蕉

Before the white mums
hesitating for a while—
the scissors

Buson

白菊に
しばしたゆとう
鋏かな

蕪村

In the candle-flame
I can see the wind—
winter snow

Ryōta

灯火を
見れば風あり
冬の雪

蓼太

Early summer rain—
a letter from home
arrives damp

Haritsu

五月雨や
故郷の手紙
ぬれて着く

杷栗

The laughter
of workers—
  a single color
    Hakushi

労働者
ただ一色の
笑い声
  伯史

Men, women
and their shadows—
    dancing
      Santōka

おとこおんなと
その影も
おどる
    山頭火

Lost on the road—
so just there
I stopped
Santōka

まようた道で
そのまま
止まる
山頭火

Cold moon—
feeling the pebbles
under my shoes
Buson

寒月や
小石のさわる
沓の底
蕪村

Amid tree shadows
my own shadow moves—
winter moon

Shiki

木の影や
我が影動く
冬の月
　　子規

What heat today!
I blow the dust
  from a rock
        Onitsura

何と今日の
暑さはと石の
塵を吹く
    鬼貫

An autumn mosquito
determined to die
  bites me
          Shiki

秋の蚊や
死ぬる覚悟で
我をさす
    子規

Amid the mosquitos
taking a bath in the tub—
  temple sexton
        Haritsu

蚊の中
行水するや
寺男
    杷栗

Out from the gate,
I too am a traveler—
autumn dusk

Buson

門を出れば

我も行く人

秋の暮れ

蕪村

The beggar
wears heaven and earth
as summer clothes

Kikaku

乞食かな

天地をきたる

夏衣

其角

Lonely
after killing the spider—
evening cold

Shiki

蜘蛛殺す

後の淋しき

夜寒かな

子規

Sweeping up
the passing of spring—
fallen leaves
Buson

行く春の
尻べに掃う
落ち葉かな
蕪村

Leaning on a tree—
through sparse leaves
the starry night
Shiki

木によれば
枝葉まばらに
星月夜
子規

The warbler's voice—
and I stop
washing dishes
Chigetsu

鶯に
手も体めぬ
ながしもと
智月

Selling ladles
he shows how to scoop up
nothing at all
Anonymous

柄杓売
なんにもないを
汲んで見せ

Short summer night—
passing through the gate
two nuns
Haritsu

みじか夜の
門つりけり
尼二人
　　杷栗

Planting my buttocks
in the potato-plant leaves—
moon-viewing
Haritsu

芋の葉に
尻を据えたる
月見かな
　　杷栗

Like a will-'o-the-wisp
I enjoy my journey—
summer fields
Hokusai

ひと魂で
行く気散じゃ
夏の原
　　北斎

In the large room
one person
and one fly
Issa

人一人
はえも一つや
大座敷
　　一茶

Meditation—
facing the wall of books
on the shelf
Anonymous

面壁を
我は書棚の
書にたいす

Making sushi
and feeling lonely
for a while
          Buson

すしおして
暫くきびしき
心かな
          蕪村

Awakened
when the ice
burst the waterjar
          Bashō

瓶わるる
夜の氷の
ねざめかな
          芭蕉

No talents
also no sins—
          winter solitude
                    Issa

能なしは
罪も又なし
冬ごもり
          一茶

This autumn
no child in my lap
for moonviewing
Onitsura

この秋や
ひざに子のなき
月見かな
鬼貴

Sudden shower—
a woman looking out
alone
Otsuyū

夕立ちや
ひとり外見る
女かな
乙由

The stone-carver
cools his chisel
　　in the clear stream
　　　　　Buson

石工の
のみ冷やしたる
清水かな
　　　　蕪村

How delightful—
walking on dewy grasses
　　in straw sandals
　　　　　Haritsu

心地よく
草の露踏む
　　わらじかな
　　　　　杷栗

Only the moon and I
remain on the bridge
　　cooling off
　　　　　Kikusha

月と我と
ばかり残りぬ
橋涼み
　　　　菊舎

Cuckoo—

a monk wrote poems on a rock

and left

Haritsu

閑古鳥

僧石に詩を

題し去る

杷栗

Hearing footsteps

one shadow

becomes two

Anonymous

足音で

二つにわれる

影法師

Apricot—

that sweet-looking person

also looks sleepy

Saisei

杏

あまさうな人は

睡むさうな

犀星

Returning in heavy snow

and writing a letter

to my wife

Santōka

雪降る中を

帰り着て妻え

手紙書く

山頭火

Using a candle
to light a candle—
spring evening
            Buson

燭 の 火 を
燭 に 移 す や
春 の 夕
            蕪 村

Pear blossoms—
a woman reads a letter
by moonlight
            Buson

梨 の 花
月 に 文 読 む
女 あ り
            蕪 村

Spring rain—
the bedding still body-shaped
after I crawled out
            Shōha

春 雨 や
抜 け 出 た ま ま の
夜 着 の 穴
            召 波

Winter seclusion—
hide-and-seek even with
my wife and children
Buson

冬ごもり

妻にもこにも

かくれん坊

蕪村

Taking off the flower robe
I'm entwined in
  a myriad of sashes
           Hisa

花衣
ぬぐやまつはる
  紐いろいろ
        久

Whatever she wears
she becomes beautiful—
  moon-viewing
         Chiyo

何きても
美しうなる
  月見かな
      千代

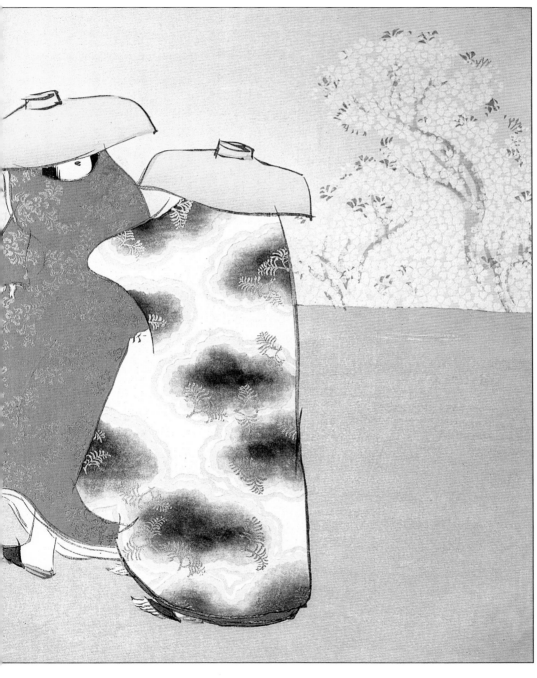

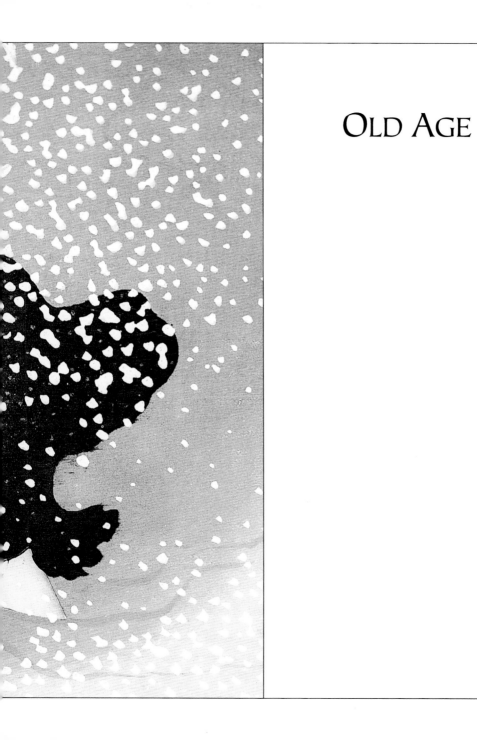

OLD AGE

Left to live on,
left to live on and on—
this cold
                    Issa

生き残り
生きのこりたる
寒さかな
              一茶

Winter rain—
I'm not dead yet
        Santōka

しぐるる
死なないでいる
            山頭火

Tilling the field
the old man's hat
        becomes crooked
                    Kitō

畑をうつ
翁が頭巾
    ゆがみけり
            几董

Walking with canes
one grey-haired family
    is visiting graves
                    Bashō

一家皆
白髪に杖や
    墓参り
            芭蕉

Early summer rain
running through the gutters—
old man's music

Buson

五月雨の
うつぼばしらや
老の耳

蕪村

Spring leisure
walking with a cane
　puttering in my garden
　　　　Issa

長閑さや
杖をついて庭を
徘徊す
　　　　一茶

Even grandma
goes out drinking—
　moonlit night
　　　　Issa

婆どのが
酒呑みに行く
月よかな
　　　　一茶

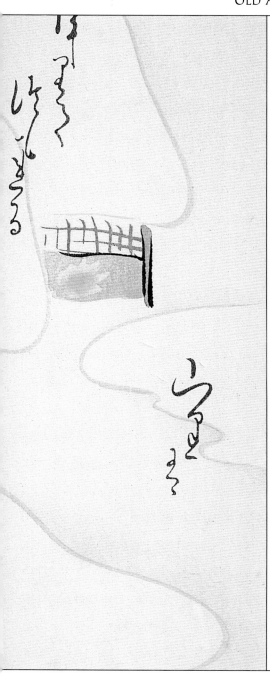

Feeling lonely
I eat my dinner—
autumn winds
Issa

さびしさに
飯をくうなり
秋のかぜ
一茶

My coughing
mixes with insect voices—
awake at night
Jōsō

虫の音の
中にせきだす
寝覚めかな
丈草

Feeling my bones
on the quilting—
night frost

Buson

我が骨の

蒲団にさわる

霜夜かな

蕪村

Colder than snow
on my white hair—
the winter moon

Jōsō

雪よりも

寒し白髪に

冬の月

丈草

Charcoal fire—
my years dwindle down
just like that

Issa

すみの火や

年のへるも

あのとうり

一茶

Spring leisure—
the swift days and months
forgotten
                    Taigi

長閑さや
早き月日を
忘れたり
          太祇

Owning nothing—
such peace,
     such coolness!
                    Issa

何もないが
心安さよ
涼しさよ
          一茶

Blossoms fallen—
people's hearts
     become quiet
               Koyū-ni

花ちりて
静かになりぬ
人心
     古友尼

Seeing that I'm old
even the mosquito whispers
closer to my ear
                    Issa

年寄りと
見てや鳴く蚊も
耳のそば
               一茶

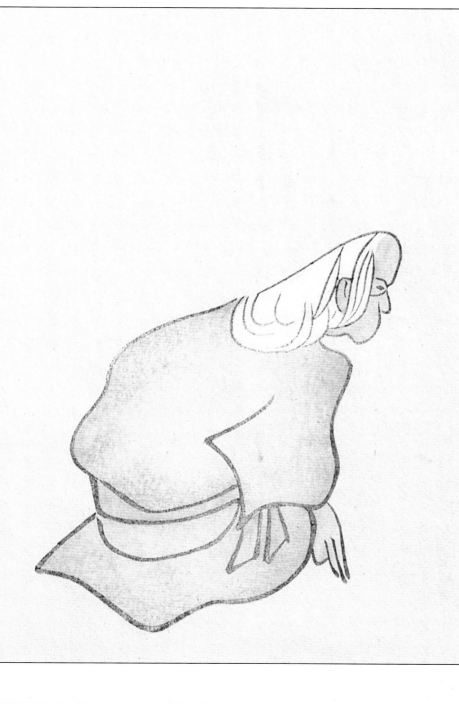

Getting colder—

no insects

come to the lamp
Shiki

やや寒み

灯による虫も

なかりけり

子規

Solitary hut—

the moon is falling

over the grasses
Shiki

家弧なり

月落ちかかる

草の上

子規

Loneliness

also has its pleasure—

autumn dusk
Buson

淋しさの

うれしくもあり

秋の暮れ

蕪村

Autumn of my years—

the moon is perfect

and yet—
Issa

身の秋や

月は無瑕の

月ながら

一茶

A single guest
visits a single host—
autumn evening
Buson

一人来て
一人訪ふや
秋の暮れ
蕪村

Without a word
the guest, the host,
white chrysanthemums
Ryōta

ものいわず
客と亭主と
白菊と
蓼太

Returning with me,
my shadow takes me home
from moonviewing
Sodō

我をつれて
我が影帰る
月見かな
素道

Finger-aching cold—
I dropped my broom
　under the pines
　　　　Taigi

つめたさに
ほうき捨てけり
　松の下
　　　　太祇

　　　　　　　　Midnight—
　　　human voices passing through
　　　　the winter cold
　　　　　　　　　Yaha

　　　　人声の
　　　夜半を逸ぐる
　　　　寒さかな
　　　　　　野坡

"Coming, coming,"
but someone still knocks—
　snowy gate
　　　　Kyōrai

応応と
言えど叩くや
　雪の門
　　　　去来

Watching
the moon fall
alone
Santōka

落ちかかる

月を見ているに

一人

山頭火

Getting old
I slip on a watermelon rind
in my dance
Sōchō

老いぬれば
西瓜にすべる
踊りかな
巣兆

This autumn
why do I feel old?
a bird in a cloud
Bashō

此秋は

何で年よる

雲に鳥

芭蕉

All of a sudden
a tooth fell out—
autumn wind
Sampu

がつくりと

抜け初むる歯や

秋の風

杉風

Flesh getting thin—
these are thick bones
Hōya

肉がやせて来る

太い骨である

放哉

Are my youthful dreams
still unfinished?
this morning's frost
Anonymous

若き夢
まだ身果てぬや
今朝の霜

Skeletons
covered with adornment—
flower viewing
Onitsura

がいこつの
うえをよそうて
花見かな

鬼貫

Taking a nap
I hide within myself—
winter seclusion
Buson

居眠りて
我はかくれん
冬ごもり

蕪村

Old man's love
when I try to forget
late autumn rain
Buson

老が恋
わすれんとすれば
しぐれかな
蕪村

Scattered snow—
with his seventy-year-old face
night soba-seller
Issa

雪ちるや
七十顔の
夜そば売
一茶

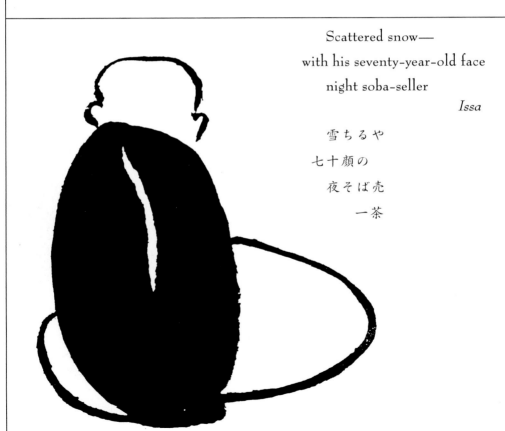

Shoulders bowed
sitting together wrapped in
     a shower of cicada voices
               Anonymous

丸き背の
よりそう包むや
蝉時雨

When I finally die—
wild grasses,
     rain falling
               Santōka

死んでしまえば
雑草
     雨ふる

          山頭火

THE ARTISTS

Chō Gesshō (1772–1832) A native of Hikone, Gesshō became one of the most famous artists of Nagoya, painting in a style that mixed literati and more naturalistic styles.

Hakuin Ekaku (1685–1768) Considered the most important Zen Master of the past five hundred years, Hakuin was also the greatest later Zen painter, creating a large number of works with power, humor, and incisive brushwork.

Hanabusa Itchō (1652–1724) A leading painter who trained in the Kanō School, Itchō displayed a special wit and humor in much of his work.

Ikeno Taiga (1723–76) One of the great literati painters, Taiga was unusual in that he displayed his art fully at a youthful age, creating some of the most imaginative and delightful of all Japanese paintings.

Iwake Nangai (dates unknown) Also called Kimbei, Nangai worked in Nagoya in the early nineteenth century.

Iwasa Matabei (1578–1650) After studying both the courtly Tosa and the official Kanō painting traditions, Matabei painted a number of genre scenes; he is credited as being a forerunner of the ukiyo-e ("floating world") style of art.

Kakudō (dates unknown) Kakudō was one of a number of artists ocntributing to the woodblock books in decorative style during the Meiji Period (1868-1912).

Kamisaka Sekka (1866–1942) Although his work has only recently become widely known, Sekka was one of the greatest designers and artists of modern Japan, and his many designs for woodblock books are especially splendid.

Katsushika Hokusai (1760–1849) One of ther most inventive and prolific artists in Japanese history, Hokusai was especially famous for his woodblock print designs and his inveterate sketching from life.

Ki Baitei (1744–1810) One of the major painting pupils of Buson, Baitei (also known as Kyūrō) lived in Shiga Prefecture and created both bold landscapes and humorous figure studies.

Matsumura Goshun (1752–1811) A leading pupil of Buson, Goshun changed his painting style midway through his career from the Chinese-derived literati style to the more naturalistic manner of Maruyama Ōkyo.

Mikuma Katen (1730–94) After studying painting with Gekko in Nagasaki, Katen lived in Kyoto as both artist and haiku poet.

Miyoshi Bokushō (dates unknown) A Nagoya artist, Bokushō was probably a pupil of Chō Gesshō.

Ogata Kōrin (1658–1716) One of the greatest of all decorative painters, Kōrin inspired the later artist Sakai Hōitsu, who published several books of designs by the master.

Takehara Shunshōsai (dates unknown) Working in the late eighteenth century, Shunshōsai designed many humorous pictures for woodblock books.

Tani Saidō (dates unknown) A painter from Nagoya, Saidō was commonly known as Kichibei.

Yamaguchi Soken (1759–1818) One of the major pupils of the naturalistic master Maruyama Ōkyo, Soken was especially gifted in figure subjects, as is shown by his delightful designs for woodblock books.

Yamamoto Shunkyō (1871–1933) As well as creating designs for publications of decorative art, Shunkyō was considered one of the founders of the modern Kyoto school of painting.

Yosa Buson (1716–83) A rare master in that he was equally great at both painting and haiku poetry.

Yūzan (dates unknown)

THE POETS

Bashō (1644–94) Widely admired as the greatest of all haiku masters, Bashō left samurai life at the age of twenty-five to devote himself to poetry. He made several journeys that he celebrated in combinations of prose and haiku called *haibun,* and his deep humanity and depth of spirit influenced Japanese literature profoundly.

Buson (1716–83) One of the greatest masters of haiku, Buson was also a leading painter in the literati school, with a warmth of vision that is apparent in both arts.

Chigetsu (1634?–1708?) A pupil of Bashō, Chigetsu was one of the most famous poets of her era; after her husband died in 1638, she became a Buddhist nun. Her son Otokuni also became a fine haiku poet.

Chiyo (1703–75) Beginning to write haiku on her own at the age of fifteen, Chiyo later studied with Shikō and eventually became a nun. Her haiku style achieved great popularity with its direct expression and witty mastery of language.

Gyōtai (1732–92) A poet from Nagoya, Gyōtai attempted to bring haiku to the excellence of Bashō and Buson at a time when the poetic form was becoming more clever and superficial.

Hakushi (dates unknown) A writer from Edo (Tokyo) of humorous verse.

Haritsu (1865–1944) Born in the small town of Shingū in Wakayama, Fukuda Haritsu became a pupil of Shiki in Tokyo, then moved to Kyoto, where he led the life of a scholar-poet using the name Kodōjin (Old Taoist). He wrote haiku, *waka,* and Chinese-style poetry, and painted both *haiga* and literati landscapes.

Hisa (1890–1946) A poet in the coterie of Takahama Kyoshi, Sugita Hisa married a painter. Her haiku style has a rich romantic flavor.

Hokusai (1760–1849) Known as one of the greatest artists and print-designers in Japanese history, Hokusai also occasionally composed haiku.

Hōya (1885–1941) Spending his life working at temples, Ozaki Hōya wrote haiku noted for their free form and direct language.

Issa (1762–1826) A poet whose life was filled with personal tragedy, Issa became the most compassionate of all haiku masters, with a special feeling for children.

Jōsō (1662–1704) Due to poor health, Jōsō gave up his samurai position at the age of twenty-six and became a monk. He studied haiku with Bashō, and after the death of his master lived a quiet and solitary life.

Kikaku (1661–1707) One of the leading pupils of Bashō, Kikaku was also expert in Chinese-style poetry, Confucianism, medicine, calligraphy, and painting. His poetic style is known for its wit and humor.

Kikusha (1753–1826) Born in Yamaguchi, Kikusha devoted herself to the arts, including painting, calligraphy, waka, Chinese-style verse, and haiku. After her husband died when she was twenty-four years old, she became a nun.

Kitō (1741–89) One of the leading pupils of Buson, Kitō also followed the style of Kikaku. Writing poems featuring the direct observation of daily life, he also was fond of saké; in his final years he became a monk.

Kōyō (1867–1903) Known primarily for his novels written in colloquial style such as *Golden Demon,* Kōyō was also a fine haiku poet during his short life.

Koyū-ni (active late eighteenth century) A woman of Edo (Tokyo), Koyū-ni was a pupil of Songi, who died in 1782.

Kyōrai (1651–1704) Born in Nagasaki, Kyōrai moved to Kyoto at the age of eight and studied martial arts and astronomy. He later became a pupil of Bashō, and he wrote both haiku and works about poetics that influenced later generations of poets.

Onitsura (1661–1738) Onitsura began to study haiku at the age of eight, and he became a successful poet in his teens. In 1685 he proclaimed that sincerity was the most important virtue in haiku, and thereafter wrote in a simple and straightforward style.

Otsuyū (1675–1739) Also known as Nakagawa Bakurin, Otsuyū was a poet from Ise who studied with Bashō, and also created a number of *haiga.*

Ryōta (1718–87) A pupil of Rito, Ryōta settled in Edo (Tokyo), where he became a famous haiku teacher with more than three thousand pupils.

Saisei (1889–1962) A novelist and poet from Kanazawa, Murou Saisei was very influential in establishing free modern verse in Japan.

Sampu (1647–1732) A pupil and patron of Bashō, Sampu provided the master with his famous cottage Bashō-an (Banana-Plant Hermitage).

Santōka (1881–1940) A failure in his family saké business and an alcoholic, Taneda Santōka became a monk and spent most of his final years as a wandering beggar. His freely written haiku express great simplicity and strength.

Seifu-jo (1731–1814) Born in Musashi Province, Seifu studied with Chōsui and Shirao. Her haiku style is often highly subjective and personal.

Senna (1651–1723) The chief priest of Honpukuji Temple, Senna was a haiku pupil of Bashō who may have given the master some lessons in painting.

Shiki (1867–1902) Despite his short life, Shiki became the most influential haiku poet and critic of the modern era, advocating a return to the poetic ideals of Buson. He was also an expert in aesthetics, *waka* poetry, and calligraphy.

Shisōshi (dates unknown) A nineteenth-century writer of humorous verse.

Shōha (died 1771) A haiku pupil of Buson, Shōha also studied Chinese-style poetry with Hattori Nankaku. When Shōha died, Buson wrote an introduction to his collected poems.

Shōhaku (1650–1722) A doctor from Ōmi, Shōhaku studied haiku with Teitoku and Bashō and wrote poems with a peaceful and serene spirit.

Sōchō (1761–1814) The son of the famous calligrapher Yamamoto Ryūsai, Sōchō became a successful artist and haiku poet in Edo (Tokyo).

Sodō (1642–1716) Born in Kai, Sodō moved to Edo (Tokyo) and became associated with Bashō.

Sōseki (1867–1916) The most famous novelist of his time, Natsume Sōseki studied in England and later taught English literature in Japan. Less known as a haiku poet, he nevertheless wrote many fine verses.

Taigi (1709–71) Born in Edo (Tokyo), Taigi moved to the entertainment district of Kyoto where he became associated with Buson.

Toshiko (dates unknown)

Yaha (1662–1740) A merchant from Fukui, Yaha traveled to Edo (Tokyo) and became a haiku pupil of Bashō, who admired his lightness of touch.

THE ILLUSTRATIONS

of Recent Eccentrics, 1790), Eccentric in the Fields

p. 100 Yosa Buson, *Yahan-ō Haisenchō* (Haiga Poets by Yahan-ō, 1911), Poet from Behind

p. 101 Yosa Buson, *Yahan-ō Haisenchō* (Haiga Poets by Yahan-ō, 1911), Poet in Profile

page 102 Yōzan, *Shinzuan* (New Designs, 1892), Dancing

The "Weathermark" identifies this book as a production of Weatherhill, Inc., publishers of fine books on Asia and the Pacific. Editorial supervision: Jeffrey Hunter. Book design and typography by Liz Trovato. Color separations, printing, and binding by Oceanic Graphic Printing, Hong Kong. The typefaces used are Bernhard Modern for the text and Tiepolo Book for the display.